WROTE BY **RICHARD ALLIN** COLYUMNIST

DRAWED BY **GEORGE FISHER** EDTORAL CARTOONIST

AS PUBLISHED IN THE IRE TOWN COLYUM
IN THE

Arkansas ☙ *Gazette.*

ROSE PUBLISHING COMPANY
Little Rock, Arkansas

DEDICATION

This book is dedicated, with special thanks, to members of the Arkansas General Assembly—and to legislators in Texas, Oklahoma, Louisiana, Mississippi, Tennessee, Alabama, Georgia, Florida, South Carolina, North Carolina, Virginia, West Virginia, and sometimes Kentucky and Missouri, who speak the same language.

Copyright 1983 by Richard Allin and George Fisher.

ISBN No. 0-914546-50-3

4th Printing

FOREWORD

English as used in the halls of Southern legislatures has a richness and texture quite lacking in general assemblies of other states. It makes little difference whether you hear the language in the legislative halls of Georgia or Alabama, Mississippi or Arkansas. The vocabulary and pronunciation are virtually the same.

The words in this little dictionary were taken mostly from the mouths of Arkansas's legislators, because the compiler is a columnist for the Arkansas Gazette in Little Rock in whose pages the vocabulary first appeared as a series of "lessons" for freshmen legislators.

The drawings are by the political cartoonist of the same newspaper. Both are Southerners and speak the language fluently. It is hoped that this work will assist those from other parts of the world who visit the southern states, and particularly their legislatures, to understand what's going on.

It's not always easy.

Persons trying to learn Southern legislative English should lip read the words in lexicon, then make an effort to pronounce them out loud. Finally, each should be used in a sentence. Helpful sentences are provided after many of the words in the lexicon.

A

Afore: before. "Fellers, we're gettin' the horse afore the cart with this bill."

Agin: to be opposed. "It's agin my principles to spote this minmun."

All she wrote: the end of it. "He crossed the guvnor wunst too often and that was all she wrote with the bills he was trying to get passed."

Arn: ferrous metal; (v.) press clothes.

Arthur Rightus: a disease of the bone joints, named for its discoverer. "Senator Cudwell missed the committee meeting so he could ast his chiropractor to discuss Arthur Rightus."

Ast: to put a question to, to petition. "I'll ast for his resignation."

Ast: past tense of ast. "I ast for it, and got it."

Arthured:

I WANT TO AST A QUESTION FROM THE MAN THAT **ARTHURED** THIS BILL

Arthurized: to give official permission.

Afixinto: preparing to do something. "I'm afixinto start back to the house."

An' em: anybody additional, from one to an infinite number. "I'm going with Uncle Bud an' em."

B

Babdist: opposite of Methodist. "The Babdist members of the legislature will be provided with a non-owkeehawlic fruit punch at the shindig."

Bar: seek and receive a loan of money or object. "Let me bar a cigaret . . ."

Baskibaw: state's second favorite sport.

Battree: device to store electrical energy.

Bidness:

GOVERNOR BOTTOMSLY TRIES TO RUN THE STATE LIKE A **BIDNESS**

Been to Memphis:

THEY SAY HE'S **BEEN TO MEMPHIS**

YEAH – HE'S BEEN EVERWHUR AWRIGHT

Bob War: fencing to keep the cows in.

Brother: any protestant minister.

C

Chanst: opportunity. "It ain't got no chanst o' passing."

Cheer: piece of furniture with a single seat.

Cheese: (treated as plural) cured milk curd. "Did you get a bite of them cheese?"

Crischul: fine glass. "Senator Nosegay suffered a broke ankle when he fell from the the crischul chandelier."

Chester drawers: furniture, usually wooden, to hold shirts and underwear.

Chewnbakker: Red Man, Brown's Mule, Beech-Nut.

Chimbley: smokestack. "She smoked like a chimbley."

Clean on to Memphis: all the way. "She was settin' in such a way that you couldn't hep but see clean on to Memphis."

Clear-a-fy:

THIS LANGUAGE ORTA BE **CLEARAFIED** FORE WE DOPT THIS BILL!

Cobbodist: Marxist.

Colyum: a journalistic essay, a list of figgers, or posts that hold up the front of a porch. "One more colyum like 'at and we ought to ban him from the House floor."

Come down the pike: appear, usually at random. "He ain't the onliest jaybird to come down the pike."

Compelsory: same as mandantory. "This minmun won't do no good unless we make it compelsory."

Constooshnul: basically legal; approximate opposite of unconstooshnul.

Cordnate: to bring into common action. "Senator Bumbaugh and Reppazentative Lurton will cordnate the joint action."

Corntrak: a binding agreement.

Corum court: a county legislative and levying body.

Cotton to: take a liking to; behave obsequiously toward.

County excessor: a fiscal officer.

Culbert: a drainage structure. "His company subcontracted the culberts on the viadock project."

D

Decative: ornamental

Deef: unable to hear.

Deerleck: unguided, lacking. "Let's not be deerleck in ire duty."

Dest: piece of furniture for work and writing. "Genmuns, let's return to your dests afore the next vote."

Diffunce: variance, dissimilarity. "They ain't a dime's worth of diffunce between 'em."

Dinner: the noon hour, also, lunch.

Dite:

Doan: Does not. "Hit doan matter."

Done: past tense of did. "He done it, shore as the world."

Do What?: reply to almost any question not understood. Can be used for "huh?", "please repeat that," "where?", "how?", or "who are you?" "Senator, I'd like to introduce my mother?" "Do what?"

Drank: an imbibable beverage; (v.) to imbibe a beverage.

Dreckly: soon, before long. "We'll vote on your minmun dreckly, Senator Lurton."

Dreen:

THEM TAX EVADERS ARE GONNA **DREEN** THE STATE TREASURY DRY!

Dry County: a political subdivision where alcoholic beverages are also sold on Sundays.

E

Ecksettera: abbreviation for et cetera. "The Quorum Court will not give us enough money for supplies, equipment, ecksettera."

Electorial: as cast by official electors, such as the Electorial College.

Ellum: stately shade tree.

Emetrius: retired, with a title corresponding to that held in active service. "I'd like to introduce Dr. Morbed Pipkin, president emetrius of Riceland Community College."

Eench: 1-12th of a foot.

Ejicate: school, teach.

English: an optional college course.

Envellup: enclosure for a letter.

Esplane: elucidate.

Exculating: rising, increase. "The costs of operations have been exculating."

Extry: additional, more than needed. "This here proprashun has so many extries until I'll not be able to vote for it."

Excape: to get away. "He nearly excaped."

Enthusanasia: mercy death.

Eyedee: concept, thought. "That's the best eyedee yet to come down the pike."

F

Fangar: a digit, part of the hand to point with.

Far: to dismiss from a job.

Far: flame.

Far tar:

Farst: timber, woods.

Feddle: relating to the national gubment. "The feddle gubment has took over all the purrogatives of the state."

Fem: light-sensitive materal for taking pitchers.

Fewnl: last rites with interment.

Flashy: hefty, overweight.

Flire: rose, daisy, etc.

Flire: basic ingredient of bread.

Frivolunt: trivial. "This year's a frivolunt motion."

Figgers: numbers.

Futbaw: the purpose of the state university.

Fur: preposition.

Fur: distance. "How fur is it?"

Furn: alien.

G

Garntee: certify, assure. "I'll garntee you one dang thang!"

Genl Semly: the state legislature.

Gentile: Babdist, Methodist.

Goin' to the house: heading for home.

Git to Whur: arrive at.

Got to whur: arrived at. Gonna git to whur. Will eventually occur. "It's gonna git to whur we won't be able to walk outn these halls without being costed by a homasexul."

Gubment:

THE **GUBMENT** HAS TOOK OVER ALL THE PURROGATIVES OF THIS STATE

H

Hanius: particularly offensive or revolting. "It was a hanius crime."

Har: to employ. "They harred him one day, farred him the next."

Har education: college.

hell far: (mild oath.) Darn!

Hep: to assist. (There are some Southern counties where the inhabitants are incapable of pronouncing an interior "l" in a word.) "This line item will arthurize the Revenue Department to har extry hep."

Hern: feminine possessive pronoun. "They taken it though it wasn't hern."

Het Up: agitated, irritated.

Hire Yew?:

Hote Tell: a lodging. "This bill would make it illegal for any hote tell withing two hundred yards of a church to sell owkeehawlic beverages."

Hisn: masculine possessive pronoun. "He said the car wasn't hisn, but the trooper arrested him anyway."

Hunnud: written 100.

I

Ifn: if.

I-moana:

Incarcinate: to put behind bars. "Senator Bambaugh was wrongly incarcinated by a trooper who mistook the Senator's ailment for intoxication."

Ink pen: writing instrument.

Innerduce: to present, bring up. "I'd like to innerduce Mizzrizz Lester Darnell, president of the Laptown Cultural Club."

Ire: division of time. "There ain't enough ires in the day to get this year work done."

Irrepable: not correctable. "This bill 'll do irrepable damage to the teacher re ment system as we know it."

Irrevelant. revelant.

J

Jannyerry: first month.

Jerden: Biblical river.

K

Kep: held, detained, or retained. "This news should not of been kep from him."

Kindly: sort of. "This proprashun is kindly large for something no more important than the Fine Arts Department."

THE PROPRASHUN IS **KINDLY** LARGE FOR SOMETHING NO MORE IMPORTANT THAN THE FINE ARTS DEPARTMENT

L

Led: top, cover. "This bill will put a led on spending."

Liberry: building full of books, sometimes found on state college campuses.

Look and a holler: a moderate distance. Two looks and a holler: A long walk.

Lysuns (always plural): a permit to operate or act. "When the game warden ast for my lysuns, I couldn't find them."

M

Manaze: a salad and sandwich dressing.

Mandantory: required, compelsory. "This is a mandantory provision."

Marker: pencil. "Loan me yur marker, Senator."

Markin:

ROY LEE'S A REAL PATRIOTIC CITIZEN

YEAH HE'S A TRUE BLUE **MARKIN** AWRIGHT

Mater: red round vegetable, often sliced and garnished with manaze.

News Item: Gov. Bagby foresees time when the legislature will be meeting year-round.

Maxium: the most.

Mess of: a goodly amount. "We got a mess of bills to work on."

Mend:

Minner: fish bait.

Mostest: the greatest amount or number. "This is the mostest we have ever been ast to proprate for a retarment plan."

Mote tell: motor hote-tell.

Minium: the least.

Mischeevious: impish.

Missreppazent: mislead, as to fact. "The lobbyist missreppazented hisself such that I almost didn't let him buy mu dinner."

Mite: a small amount.

Mizzrizz: (written Mrs.)

I'D LIKE TO INTRODUCE THE SIXTH GRADE CLASS FROM DUTCH ELLUM ELEMENTARY SCHOOL WITH THEIR TEACHER **MIZZRIZZ FOSTORIA GULLET!**

CLAP CLAP CLAP CLAP

Morning ire: first part of daily session when non-controversial measures are considered.

N

Nar: not wide, thin. "He's too nar headed to have good sense."

Narly: by the skin of one's teeth.

Newqueler: energy generated from splitting of the atom. "The committee chairman ast if the Air Force had to pay county taxes on their newqueler warheads."

Non-constooshnul: illegal, baseless.

O

Oakree: slimy vegetable, served boiled with butter, or fried. An acquired taste.

Onliest: the single one, unique. "He thinks he's the onliest frog in the pond."

Orditor: state fiscal official.

Ort: should. "It's sompn we ort to do now, afore a day goes by.

Ovair:

Owkeehaw: beverage spirits. "L'il lady, take a drank. Hit doan contain no owkeehaw."

TAKE A DRANK, LIL LADY – HIT DOAN CONTAIN NO **OW-KEE-HAW!**

Oyschur: succulent shellfish, served on the half shell or fried. "Reppazentative Lester Postelle, an ordained fundamentalist minister, declined to eat the oyschurs because they are not mentioned in the Bible."

P

Pamplet: booklet containing message or essay. "Mr. Speaker, we're being unindated with pamplets."

Partial post: a mailing category. "It'll be right smart cheaper to send it partial post."

Peculiary: particular. "These is peculiary times that calls for suppamental funds to meet emergencies."

Peel: medicine in a small dose. "I taken my blood peel which sometimes makes me stagger a little."

Peerogatives: rights and privileges.

Pertickaler: specific. "This pertickaler bill ain't got no more chance't o' passing than a snowball in the Bad Place."

Physical year: a year at the end of which all financial records must be reconciled. "This won't take effect til after the physical year."

Pire:

DON'T GET ME WRONG AMY, BUT GITTIN' A BILL PAST THE BUDGET COMMITTEE GIVES A FELLER A REAL SENSE OF **PIRE**

Pire house: light plant.

Pitcher: photo. "He taken my pitcher for the paper."

Pitcher show: movie.

Plumb: completely.

Popler: generally liked; of the general public. "This was a right smart diffunce between the popler and the electorial vote."

Pronounciation: the way a word is said. "His pronounciation sounded furn."

Proprashun: the amount proprated.

Proprate:

WE'RE NOTTA GONNA **PROPRATE** NO MORE FUNDS FOR NO REMEDIAL ENGLISH CLASSES!

Puhsnel: private.

Pup wood: from which paper is made.

Pursnail: the people working for a department.

Purty: toy or small gift.

Q

Queasly: slight sick feeling.

R

Rat cheer:

THEM PAGES WAS **RAT CHEER** TIL I STARTED ALOOKIN FOR 'EM

Reckanize: to acknowledge from the chair. "You are not reckanized, Senator Tugwell, so set down!"

Reggalate: to apply rules.

Reppazent: to act in another's behalf. "The Speaker ast me who I reppazent."

Retar: withdraw from work.

Retarment: laying down the burdens of work, usually with a pension.

Revelant: germane, appropriate. "Your point idn't revelant, Reppazentative Tugwell."

Right smart: a considerable amount.

Rillaty: company that sells rillastate.

Rillastate: buildings and land. "I was ast to innerduce this bill by the rillastate brokers of my county."

Rual: (adj.) country.

Rubber: eraser.

Rurned: damaged or soiled beyond repair. "Dog if I ain't rurned this shirt."

S

Sairdy: last day of the week.

Say what?: (see Do what?)

Seerse: sober, not kidding.

The Joint Budget Committee is now in session.

Sef: one's person.

Sekkatay: assistant, stenographer.

Sfiscated: polished, urbane.

Shar: brief rain.

Sherf: county law officer.

Shine: illicitly made liquor.

Shore: certain.

Shouldahad: should have.

Shreezeport: a city in northern Louisiana.

Sire: tart tasting.

Slippers: shoes.

Spatial guest: distinguished visitor.

Spatial Session: an extraordinary meeting of the General Assembly, called by the governor for a specific purpose. "I'll bet a purty that the guvner is afixingto call a spatial session."

Splane: to clearafy.

Stadium: intellectual center of a state college or university campus.

Stass-stiss-stics: a collection of quantitative data. "It's got to whur we caint believe none of them stass-stiss-stics."

Sody cracker: saltine. "We eat sody crackers and vieenies for supper last night."

Soshayshun: a group organized for a common interest. "The hearings was attended by the Tar Dealers Soshayshun."

Spote:

THEY AIN'T GOT MUCH **SPOTE** FOR THIS PERTICKALAR MEASURE

Sprang: between winter and summer.

Stallded: interruption of operation. "He got the bill stallded in committee."

Statchit: law.

Stippalate: to agree in advance. "I'd like to stippalate that you pick up the drink check."

Strang: cotton twine, also used figuratively. "There waz no strangs attached."

Sweet milk: fresh from the cow.

Sweet tater: yam-like root vegetable.

Suppamenel: additional.

T

T'mar: day following today.

Tar: a wheel covering to provide traction and absorb shocks.

Takin' ker: being careful.

Tarred: to be fatigued, or bored. "I'm sick and tarred of this year bill."

Tater: starchy root vegetable.

Tetnical: special practical knowledge. "This bill is wrote too tetnical."

Thaddledo: enough.

Thang: item.

This year: this one. "I wisht yallud look at this year measure with a grain of salt."

Tickled: pleased. "We're tickled to have the Fifth Grade class from Willer Creek School."

Tickled to death: Very pleased.

Toe dancin' bill: any cultural measure.

Tollable: bearable, reasonable.

Tuckered: real tarred.

Tump:

JUDGE PHILPOT **TUMPED** OVER HIS CHEER

Turblist: worst. "This is the turblist tastin' fish I ever eat."

Twice-st: two times. "I never drunk moonshine but twice-st in my life."

U

Unindated:

Unloosen: loosen, untie.

Unnerstan: comprehend.

Unthaw: melt. "This popsickle done unthawed and soiled my vest."

V

Veriest: most exact, same. "That's the veriest idee I had."

Viadock: an overpass. "His car had a flat tar in the middle of the viadock."

Vettern: former service man.

Vy-EE-na: (ejicated version) canned sausage eat with sody crackers.

Vy-EE-nee: (hick version)

THEM FANCY KAF-AYS ARE NICE, TOM—BUT IT'S HARD TO BEAT **VY-EE-NEE** SAUSAGES AND CRACKERS

W

Warsh: clean with water, frequently using soap.

Warshington: capitol of the United States.

Wawst: winged stinging insect.

Whur at: what's the location?

Widder woman: woman whose husband has died. "He married a rich widder woman."

Willer: tree on a river bank.

Wrench: warsh in clear water. "I thought the shirt was rurned until I wrenched the ink offn it."

Wretch: past tense of reach.

Wrop: enclose and tie in paper or cloth.

Wunst: one time. "If he done it wunst he done it a thousand times."

XYZ

Y'all: (always used in plural) You (pl.)

Yellow: a telephone greeting. "Yellow . . . yes, this is him."

Yestiddy: day before today.

Yourn: second person possessive pronoun. "Is this yourn? No. It's hisn."

You-uns (or You-unses, pl.): persons being addressed.

Yonder: ovair.

The gas bubble having subsided and a melt-down avoided, the Legislature has adjourned.

This book is hilarious. I want more copies. Send me _____ copies of *Southern Legislative Dictionary* for $4.95 each. Remittance is enclosed. Send To:

Name_____

_____

Street Address_____

_____

City _____

State _____ Zip_____

ROSE PUBLISHING COMPANY
301 Louisiana
Little Rock, AR 72201